Paul Newman

Table of Contents

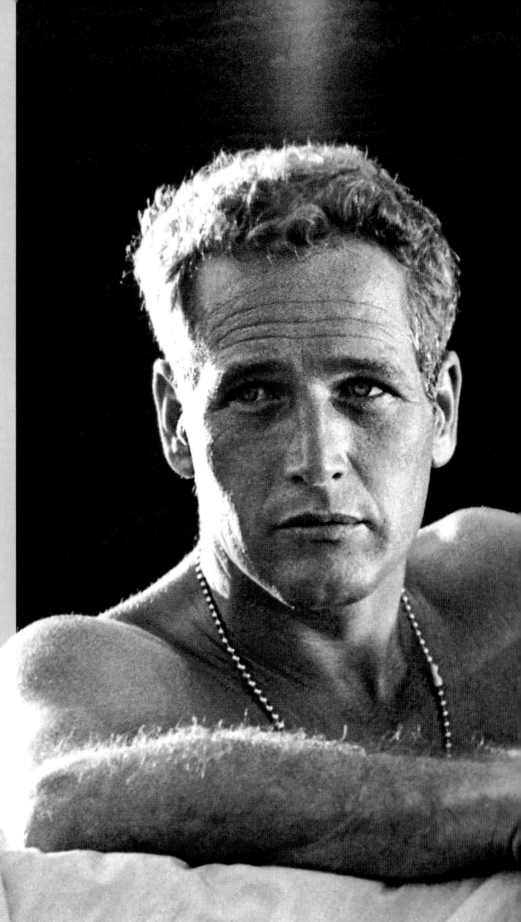

Remembering Paul Newman

He was an actor whose greatest performances—in *Hud, Cool Hand Luke, The Hustler* and *Butch Cassidy and the Sundance Kid*—became part of American culture and memory. And he was much more than that.

Smart, funny, cantankerous and kind—his Newman's Own food company raised more than $250 million for charity—Paul Newman set high standards for himself as a man and as a citizen and worked hard to live up to them. "I'd like to be remembered as a guy who tried," he once said. "Tried to be a part of his times, tried to help people communicate with one another, tried to find some decency in his own life, tried to extend himself as a human being. . . . You've got to try, that's the main thing."

As the stories and pictures on the following pages show, he succeeded.

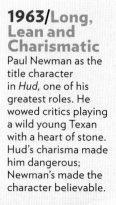

1963/Long, Lean and Charismatic
Paul Newman as the title character in *Hud*, one of his greatest roles. He wowed critics playing a wild young Texan with a heart of stone. Hud's charisma made him dangerous; Newman's made the character believable.

Cool

What is it? Hard to say. But one thing
is certain: Those who talk about it
don't have it. And Paul Newman never
talked about it

1967/A Rebel Takes Five

In *Cool Hand Luke*, Newman played a prisoner who bucked the system. "He was the ultimate nonconformist and rebel," said the actor. "In the Army or in jail, but still a free agent." It was a philosophy with which Newman could identify.

1958/And the Oscar doesn't go to . . .
Newman's wife, Joanne Woodward, won a Best Actress Oscar for *The Three Faces of Eve* in 1958; Newman, nominated that year for Best Actor for *Cat on a Hot Tin Roof*, had to content himself with his old "Noscar," a gag gift from the director and producer of 1956's *Somebody Up There Likes Me*.

THE SCHNEE-WISE
NOSCAR
AWARD
PAUL NEWMAN
FOR BEST PORTRAYAL
GENUINE AND LOVABLE IGNORANCE
FOOLING ALL OF THE PEOPLE

1956/The Contender

When Newman portrayed boxer Rocky Graziano in *Somebody Up There Likes Me*, some critics thought he was aping Marlon Brando in *On the Waterfront*. Actually, said Newman, Graziano later told him that Brando partly based his *Waterfront* portrayal on the famous heavyweight champ.

1963 / Seeing Eye to Eye
On the set of *Hud*, Newman, then 37, engaged one of the locals in a staring contest. We're betting the buzzard lost.

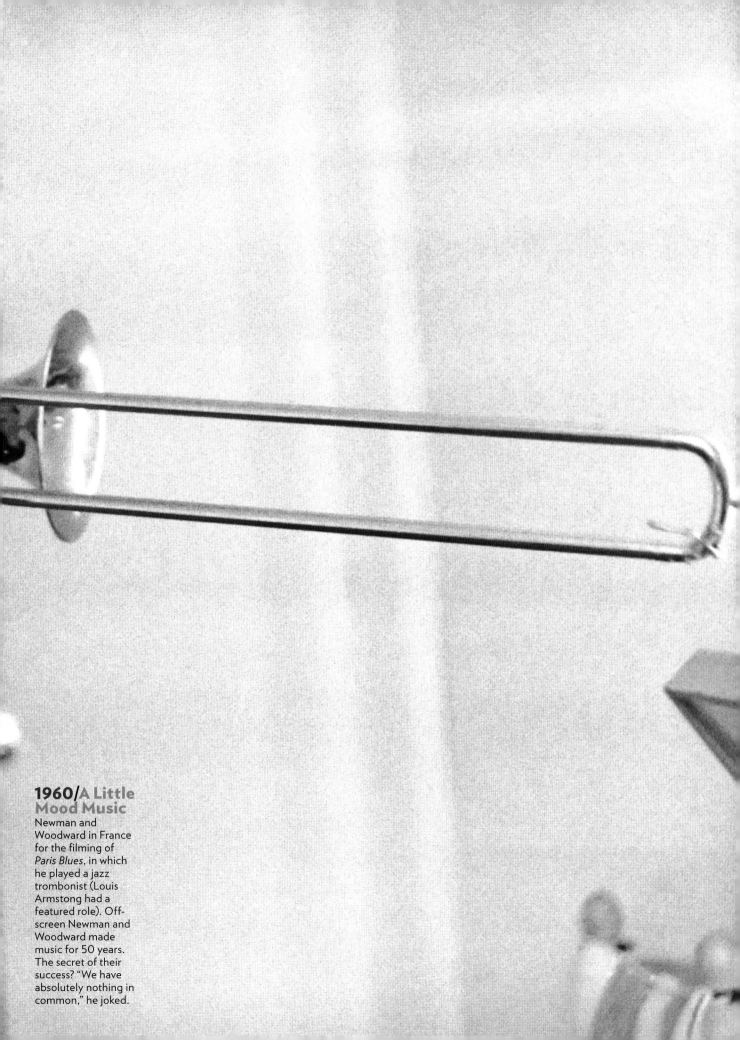

1960/A Little Mood Music
Newman and Woodward in France for the filming of *Paris Blues*, in which he played a jazz trombonist (Louis Armstong had a featured role). Off-screen Newman and Woodward made music for 50 years. The secret of their success? "We have absolutely nothing in common," he joked.

1968 / The Suburbans
"It wasn't easy living with Sam Superstar," Woodward once said. "Oh, I think Sam was pretty easy," Newman noted. "It was me that was hard."

1965/
**Motorcycle
Man**
Newman (on the
set of *Harper*) loved
anything with wheels.
In New York, he com-
muted to Broadway
by Vespa because he
found it faster than
a cab. But he crashed
one of his bikes in
1965, badly injuring
his hand, and sold
his three motorcycles
the next day.

With Joanne
On the town (at the sort of event he rarely attended and, when he did, often left early); as a model husband (below); and doing the Frug—or is that the Watusi?—at home in 1965.

1967/A Man at Peace
It's true: The actor (boating in Florida) enjoyed a beer, or three, now and again. He admitted that his drinking got out of hand in the '60s ("hanging from chandeliers was not out of the question"), which prompted him to give up hard liquor.

On Screen

Paul Newman's remarkable face—which made him a natural leader
among Hollywood's leading men—came close to
stopping time, but his talent aged into something far greater

P

Paul Newman had one of the greatest faces in the history of Hollywood, yet he fell flat on it in his first movie in 1954. In a critically derided religious epic called *The Silver Chalice*, he was cast as a sculptor commissioned to create a chalice to enshrine Jesus' cup from the last supper. Newman, *The New York Times* wrote, "bears a striking resemblance to

Marlon Brando, but his contribution is hardly outstanding. . . . He is given mainly to thoughtful posing and automatic speech-making. And, despite the fact that he is desired by the extremely fetching Helena and the wistful Deborra, his wife, he is rarely better than wooden in his reaction to these fairly spectacular damsels." When the film appeared on TV years later, Newman, adapting the pose of cool, clear-eyed amusement that became a signature of some of his best work, took out an ad in *Variety* apologizing.

At any rate, Newman was not wooden. With every feature—brow, lips, arguably even eyelids—seemingly chiseled in stone, he looked like an antique Roman bust with the pupils painted a riveting Technicolor blue. There was, to many, no

man more handsome in the last 50 years of American moviemaking. As the stone aged, it weathered beautifully as well. Somehow, the critic Pauline Kael observed, Newman just became more glamorous with time. He was the best-preserved leading man since Cary Grant, and Grant retired before he was 65. Newman not only kept acting until he hit 80 (after which he did voice work, notably in the Pixar cartoon *Cars*), he evolved into an even more powerful presence: The change in his looks exposed an inner gravity, an emotional bedrock. In his lifetime he accumulated nine Oscar nominations, one win (for 1986's *The Color of Money*, costarring Tom Cruise) and two honorary statues. It was an exemplary career.

Newman came from the same feverish generation as Brando and James Dean—they were all in the

1967/Cool Hand Luke

The prison drama was an achievement worthy of any great male star, and a career pinnacle, but Newman modestly wondered if he lacked the emotional facets of an Olivier: "I seem to have run out of my own skin fairly early."

> "To be a good actor, you have to be a child. But who wants to take a lot of credit for being a child when you're nearly 60?"

groundbreaking era of Method acting that brought to movies a new (and now standard) vitality. (You can find a clip on YouTube showing Dean and Newman in a joint screen test for 1955's *East of Eden*.) But Newman was, in the beginning of his career, at a disadvantage compared to these guys: They were extraordinarily sexy, and they were as visceral as meat. Newman instead had flawless pulchritude—which was not the same thing.

Even though Newman went on to prove his *Silver Chalice* critics wrong as boxer Rocky Graziano in 1956's *Somebody Up There Likes Me* and pool player Fast Eddie Felson in 1961's *The Hustler*, classical good looks and emotional volatility made for a complicated mix. In one of his most famous movies, 1963's *Hud,* he plays an amoral, boozy rancher's son, a rotten, bed-hopping bastard who one drunken night comes close to raping the housekeeper. Newman doesn't try to make Hud sympathetic. He is awful, selfish, unredeemed to the end. It's a courageous performance, even 45 years later, an indelible antihero. What distracts, though, is how Newman wears a white shirt with jeans, and how in a flat, wide, black-and-white landscape this ensemble has an immaculate crispness that defies dust and cattle.

Newman, of course, realized his looks could overshadow his skill and seriousness. And yet he did not do what many actors do to prove their talent: He did not shave his head, gain weight, pitch his voice strangely. He kept in shape. (He did so many stomach crunches on a new slant board he gave himself a hernia.) He may simply have been too astute not to realize that negating his looks would just have been a different way of calling attention to them—or that, at the height of his days as a star, they were too valuable. When handsome actors like Johnny Depp cultivate eccentricities today, they are taking their cue from the great but profligate Brando, not Newman.

Newman's stardom, in fact, followed the opposite arc of Brando's: As he matured as an actor, he became more economical, paring down his performances, lowering the temperature. Looking back on even as well-regarded a performance as the one he gave in *The Hustler,* he saw evidence of trying too hard, letting the audience see him work. He changed that. A Newman performance became something cool, understated, effortless-looking and somehow a perfect fit with his looks.

2

3

5

1/Cat on a Hot Tin Roof (1958) The drama (with Elizabeth Taylor) brought Oscar nomination No. 1.
2/The Life and Times of Judge Roy Bean (1972) The Western lowlife was a favorite role.
3/Somebody Up There Likes Me (1956) He trained in the ring to play Rocky Graziano.
4/The Hustler (1961) He admitted it "really hurt" to lose the Oscar as Fast Eddie Felson.
5/The Sting (1973) Like *Sundance*, his Redford reunion was, at the time, one of the Top 10 grossing films ever.

4

1986/The Color of Money

"It's not only dangerous to repeat yourself, it's damned tiresome," Newman said. But he couldn't resist reprising one of his greatest roles, *The Hustler*'s Fast Eddie—and the Martin Scorsese-directed drama finally won him the acting Oscar.

His greatest popular successes were the casual buddy movies he made with another sensationally good-looking star, Robert Redford: 1969's *Butch Cassidy and the Sundance Kid*, a hip Western that now seems nostalgic and innocently silly (Newman puts Katharine Ross on the handlebars of a bicycle for an extended sequence as B.J. Thomas sings "Raindrops Keep Fallin' on My Head") and 1973's *The Sting*, which won the Best Picture Oscar. There is more of Newman-Redford than Frank Sinatra-Dean Martin in the Clooney-Pitt remake of *Ocean's Eleven*.

Oddly enough, Newman was never a real romantic lead in the same way as Redford or Warren Beatty. There is no Newman *Out of Africa* or *The Way We Were*. It simply didn't seem to be in his superstar's chemistry—he was ideally paired with Elizabeth Taylor for 1958's *Cat on a Hot Tin Roof,* although the perverse joke in that script was that his character was sexually repulsed by hers.

His most frequent costar was his wife, Joanne Woodward, a lovely, naturalistic actress whom he directed—with great sensitivity—in several movies, notably 1968's *Rachel, Rachel.* Woodward seemed happy to let her husband be the sex symbol.

Which he remained for a very long time. But as he moved deep into what are now thought of as the AARP years, he became one of the most impressively dependable actors around. The famous eyes began to reflect subtler emotions as he played gray-haired men of experience: long-nursed wounds, gruff power held in check. He finally won an Oscar in 1986 reprising the role of an older Eddie Felson in *The Color of Money,* but it was hard not to suspect it was a delayed prize for his superb turn as an alcoholic lawyer in 1982's *The Verdict*—possibly his best performance.

Any of the movies in this later curve of his career are worth watching for his acting: the Coen brothers' baffling comedy *The Hudsucker Proxy,* the rough-edged but charming portrait of small-town life *Nobody's Fool,* the L.A. noir *Twilight,* the gangster drama *The Road to Perdition* and, with Joanne Woodward, *Mr. & Mrs. Bridge*. There he gave an unforgettable performance as a proper Midwestern lawyer who shows practically no emotion whatsoever.

It was, perhaps, the ultimate Paul Newman turn—richly minimalist.

Butch Cassidy and the Sundance Kid

The outlaw dramedy romance Western set the standard for buddy movies

1969/Who *are* those guys?
Robert Redford (Sundance) and Newman (Butch) were far better looking and a lot less violent than the real bad guys. During filming, the real Butch's sister Lula Parker Betenson, then 84, visited the set and told Newman he was doing a good job.

The film's still photos (below) were inspired by real images of Sundance and his girlfriend during a visit to New York City. According to director George Roy Hill, during filming, a stuntman balked at some of the bicycle tricks he was asked to perform. Just then, Newman himself went rolling by, balanced on one foot on the bicycle's seat. Hill turned to the stuntman and said, "You're fired." A huge hit, *Butch and Sundance* grossed more than $100 million and won four Academy Awards. Newman always regretted that the outlaws died in the end, making a sequel problematical. "Those two guys," he said, "could have gone on forever." Four years later, Newman and Redford reteamed for *The Sting*—an even bigger hit.

The Sexiest Ping-Pong Players Alive?

Newman and Redford (during a shooting break) thrived on practical jokes. Mocking Newman's racing obsession, Redford sent him a wrecked Porsche. Newman had it crushed into a cube and spirited into Redford's living room.

Agua Hedi

Cool Hand Luke

One of Hollywood's most enduring antiheroes cemented Newman's image of cool, understated power

1967/You're Not the Boss of Me
Thanks to a great script and memorable shots (opposite), the image of Luke, the proto-rebel, has "been growing like some gigantic mushroom" for 40 years, said Newman.

Menace
In *Luke's* most famous line, a warden (Strother Martin), having knocked Newman into a ditch, announces, "What we've got here is failure to communicate."

And Now for Some
Completely

The Towering Inferno, a big-budget, mass-market
disaster movie, was a notable departure for Newman,
but proved a box office hit

thing
Different . . .

Inferno offered Newman front-and-center in a crazy-quilt all-star cast (Fred Astaire *and* O.J. Simpson?). Why did he make it? "You're not gonna get a sensible answer," he once said, "from a fella who put a 351-cubic-in. Ford engine in a Volkswagen."

Silver and Gold

Wow—what a sunset. Newman, from middle age on, wasn't just getting older. He was getting fantastic

"I can't think of anything that gets better with aging," Newman once said. "I'm not mellower, I'm not less angry, I'm not less self-critical, I'm not less tenacious. Maybe the best part is that your liver can't handle those beers at noon anymore. I can't think of the worst part, either. Oh, you can't get to the net as quickly. So what? It's not of consequence."

But one thing that did get better was Newman himself: Once the big star parts were no longer automatically coming his way—buddy Robert Redford was offered *The Verdict* first—he became more liberated as an actor, turning in one critically lauded turn after another. "It's a wonderfully funny, canny performance," the *New York Times'* Vincent Canby wrote of his Oscar-winning work in *The Color of Money*, "set off by the actor's intelligence that shines through the character without upstaging it." That goes for just about everything in his glorious final stretch.

Newman's last on-camera role (with beard) was for HBO's *Empire Falls* in 2005 (right). In the years leading up to that sign-off, he was an evil crime boss (with Tom Hanks) in 2002's *Road to Perdition* (left); a foulmouthed hockey player in 1977's *Slap Shot* and a cop in 1981's *Fort Apache the Bronx* (with Ken Wahl).

And as you may not

2

remember him . . .

6

7

The

1958 / Blame it on the bossa nova?
Shimmying suavely with Joan Collins in *Rally 'Round the Flag, Boys!*

"

Acting is like letting your pants down. You're exposed"

1956 The Prisoner
In *The Rack*, Newman's character faced court-martial after collaborating with the enemy while brainwashed, in a Korean POW camp.

1954 / *The Silver Chalice*
At least the camel was smiling: One critic said that Newman, as a Greek artisan named Basil, "delivered his lines with the emotional fervor of a New York Central train conductor announcing local stops." When *Chalice* aired on TV in L.A., Newman took out an ad in *Variety* that said, "Paul Newman apologizes every night this week."

Turkey

Newman nearly KO'd his career with his very first film, a biblical box office bomb called *The Silver Chalice*

The Clinch!

Pounding hearts! Weak knees! Early on, the studios worked hard to market Newman as everywoman's virile dream

1958 Feeling the Itch
On a break from shooting bad guys, Newman enjoyed a roll in the hay with Lita Milan in *The Left Handed Gun*, a Western he was proud of that had, he said, an extended life in French art-house theaters.

1962/ Bill & Coo
Newman, as drifter Chance Wayne, tries to reconcile with hometown girlfriend Heavenly Finley (Shirley Knight) in Tennessee Williams' *Sweet Bird of Youth*.

1963/ Sommer Break
"He ordered a martini...kissed a girl... and was plunged into a nightmare of danger!" So went the promo line for *The Prize*, in which Newman (with Elke Sommer) played a Nobel-winning author.

On the Set

In more than 50 years and 60 films, Newman had a lot of time between takes to make friends and plot practical jokes

**1974/
Where's
the Fire?**
Newman was
a chameleon:
Depending on the
era, the light and
his haircut, he could
look like Steve
McQueen (with him
on the set of *The
Towering Inferno*),
Marlon Brando
or James Dean.

1 In Charge Newman took to directing early and was nominated for a Best Picture Oscar for *Rachel, Rachel*.
2 Rally 'Round the Piano A break during the filming of *Rally 'Round the Flag, Boys!*
3 The Joker Goofing around on the set of *Hombre*. Newman, who loved practical jokes, once sawed director George Roy Hill's desk in half and, while filming *Buffalo Bill*, filled Robert Altman's trailer with 300 live chicks.
4 The Director Filming *Rachel, Rachel* with Estelle Parsons and
5 Woodward (in background), which brought both Newman and Woodward Oscar nominations.

The REVOLT OF THE DUSTY WIND BLASTED ANGELS.

> You have
> to keep things
> off-balance,
> or it's all over"

1 Exit Stage Right
Clowning with Princess Margaret, Lord Snowdon and director Alfred Hitchcock, who directed Newman in *Torn Curtain*.
2 I'm with the Chairman
Newman, Eva Marie Saint and Frank Sinatra preparing for a 1955 production of *Our Town*.
3 Va Va Voom, etc.
With Sophia Loren and David Niven at a *Lady L* party—a rare sort of appearance for Newman, who included public relations and "being seen" on his long list of "unnecessary things about Hollywood." His clear and vocal disdain, friends suggested, may have played a role in Newman's having to wait 32 years before being awarded, on his seventh nomination, a Best Actor Oscar.

In college, Newman lacked focus. His father, he said, "treated me like he was disappointed in me . . . and he had every right to be." The actor's success came after his father's death. "It has been one of the great agonies of my life," Newman said, "that he could never know."

Young Paul

How a kid from Shaker Heights, Ohio, ran away from the family sporting goods business and became a movie legend

H

1945/In the Navy Newman, 18 at enlistment, said he "got through the war on two razor blades."

He was a public figure who tried—very hard, often with humor or subterfuge, at times by any means necessary—to enjoy the simple pleasures of living a private life.

The public knew him, first and foremost, as an actor, one of the dominant stars of the last half of the 20th century. He came up with the class of '50s rebels—notably Marlon Brando and James Dean, with whom he vied for

early parts—and made his name playing charismatic, sexually charged antiheroes and schemers in *Hud, Cool Hand Luke* and *Cat on a Hot Tin Roof.* Two of his biggest hits, *Butch Cassidy and the Sundance Kid* and *The Sting,* linked him forever in the public mind with his friend and costar Robert Redford; more than 50 others—from the disaster movie *The Towering Inferno* to the delicate character study *Mr. and Mrs. Bridge*—made him a cultural force for more than 50 years, during which he was nominated for a Best Actor Oscar eight times (winning, the seventh time out, for *The Color of Money*). Rolling into his 60s, when many a graying heartthrob might panic, he launched what amounted to a second career playing older men who showed the scars from a hard-knock life in *The Verdict, Nobody's Fool* and the

HBO series *Empire Falls.* Newman seemed almost giddy about the chance to finally let go and look like a mess onscreen. "I was always a character actor," he said. "I just *looked* like Little Red Riding Hood."

Offscreen there were other Paul Newmans. One drove fast and, as often as possible, dodged cameras. Introduced to auto racing while filming 1969's *Winning,* he fell in love, went to driving school, worked his way up the amateur ranks and, among other achievements, took second place with his team at Le Mans in 1979. He could be ambivalent about acting and even his own talent ("One day I wake up and I think I'm terrific, and the next day I wake up and I think it's all junk") but was clear and passionate about his love for cars. "I don't care what anyone says about my acting," he said. "I've been humili-

1953/
Cat on a Hot Tin Hood
A newly minted Broadway baby, Newman contemplated the Music Box Theatre, where he was appearing in *Picnic*.

1955/
The Student
Fellow members of the Actors Studio included Marlon Brando, Steve McQueen and Rod Steiger. Said Newman of his approach: "It was monkey see, monkey do. Man, I just sat back there and watched how people did things and had enough sense to keep my big mouth shut."

1/The Artist as a Young Man Newman at age 12 in a local production of *St. George and the Dragon*.
2/Touché Fencing with a high school classmate.
3/The Undergrad At Kenyon College, where he played football, operated a laundry and fell in love with acting. "It was hard not to cast him in the lead of every show," said one instructor. In 2007 Newman donated $10 million to the school's drama department.
4/Quick Draw Newman (in *The Death of Billy the Kid*) often said that television dramas, shown live, had been a terrific training ground.
5/Prelude to a *Kiss* Backstage on Broadway in *Baby Want a Kiss* (1964).

ated, lied about. But they mess around with my racing—that's something else."

In later years the public met another Newman: a whimsical entrepreneur who, in tandem with his sidekick, writer A.E. Hotchner, started a food company, Newman's Own, that wound up, as of 2008, donating more than $250 million to charity. "There are three rules to starting a business," the pair said of their approach. "Fortunately, we don't know any of them." (Other unofficial Newman's Own mottoes: "If we ever have a plan, we're screwed" and "Just when things look darkest, they go black.") Perhaps his favorite cause was one he started himself: the Hole in the Wall summer camps, now operating in seven countries, that charge nothing and cater each year to the needs of more than 11,000 kids with cancer, HIV and other sometimes-terminal illnesses. The simple goal? To let the kids "raise hell and not feel different," said Newman.

To a large degree, Newman wanted exactly the same freedom for himself. He seldom gave interviews; when he did, they were more likely to promote a cause—nuclear disarmament, Gene McCarthy's presidential bid—than his career. He was deeply suspicious of the flatteries of Hollywood ("stuffing your ego to the bursting point like the liver of a Strasbourg goose," as he put it) and moved, with his wife, actress Joanne Woodward, to Westport, Conn., in 1962. More than anything, he longed to be treated, as he put it, "as if I were a stranger"—that is, like anyone else. He claimed to have stopped signing autographs after a man approached him at a urinal ("I wondered, 'What do I do with my hands? Do I wash them first and then shake…or shake and then wash up?'") and was driven to distraction by people who couldn't see beyond his famously blue eyes. "Someone will say, 'Thanks for wonderful evenings in the theater' and you feel terrific," he said. "And then some lady says, 'Take off your dark glasses. I want to see your blue eyes.' There's nothing that makes you feel more like a piece of meat." Most times, he'd try to deflect the request with humor. "I would take off my sunglasses, madam," he'd say, "but my pants would fall down."

Newman's is a remarkable legacy for anyone—and perhaps particularly for a man who got started in his career not out of a love for acting but because, as he put it, "I was running away from the family retail business." The second son of Arthur Newman, a partner in a sporting goods store, and the former Theresa Fetzer, who helped manage the business, Paul grew up in Shaker Heights, an upper-middle-class Cleveland suburb, and attended public schools. After high school, in 1943, he enlisted in the Navy and hoped to become a pilot but was disqualified when

1960/
Starting Out
Newman and
Woodward, newly
married rising stars,
in their Greenwich
Village apartment.

a test revealed he was color-blind. Newman instead spent the war as a radio man on a torpedo bomber in the Pacific—and had his first experience of what throughout his life he came to regard as "Newman's luck": On a day when his squadron suffered horrible casualties, he had been grounded because his pilot had an ear infection.

Returning from the war, he enrolled at Kenyon College in Ohio. To some degree, he may owe his career to a bar fight: A beer-fueled fracas got him booted from the football team during his sophomore year, and he turned to acting to fill his spare time. After graduating in 1949, he kept at it, performing in local repertory and summer-stock companies, where he met and soon married a fellow actress, Jacqueline Witte. When his father died, in 1950, Newman returned to Cleveland to run the family store—and was miserable. To his great relief, the business was sold a year later, and he enrolled in Yale Drama School, where, very quickly, he faced a test. "A guy who was directing Shaw's *Saint Joan* came up to me and said, 'I want you to do this,' and I said 'Sure,'" Newman recalled. "The first thing I saw in the script was that my character was supposed to be weeping offstage." He had no idea how to cry on cue, and panicked. Briefly. "What an ass," he told himself. "I drag my family with only $900 all the way to Connecticut and then think

of all the ways I can cop out." Instead he went to the boiler room in his boarding house and sat there for hours until he had figured out how to make tears flow at will. Later he rated his performance in *Saint Joan* as "probably as full and rich as anything I've done."

Impressed with the newcomer, instructors recommended he head down to New York and start auditioning. Newman immediately found work in a nascent form of entertainment—television—and, as he put it, lucked his way through an audition for the prestigious Actors Studio: "They mistook terror—which is what I felt—for performed emotion." Things began happening, fast: In 1953 he made his Broadway debut, as the guy who *doesn't* get the girl, in *Picnic*. When Newman asked the director, Josh Logan, if he could take the lead when the show went on the road, Logan turned him down with the explanation that he didn't project any sexual threat. "I've been chewing on that one for 20 years," he said years later. Newman's typically methodical response to Logan's assessment? Six hours a day in the gym and an analysis of what made a man sexy to a woman. "You can measure each woman," he concluded, "and find ways of being gallant, of listening, of crowding, of pursuing."

Within a year Newman had signed a movie contract with Warner Bros. and soon appeared in his

Globetrotter
Tipping back a
beer at a midnight
party in Paris during the
filming of *Paris Blues*.

1978/The Activist

Passionate about politics, Newman (observing a 1978 U.N. conference on nuclear disarmament) believed fame gave him both an opportunity and an obligation. "Do you abdicate the responsibilities of citizenship merely because you carry a SAG card?" he asked. "Or do you dig deeply and become as knowledgeable an expert as you can and speak your piece and hope your weight is being thrown on the right side?"

ANGOLA

UPPER VOLTA

first film, *The Silver Chalice,* a howling turkey of a costume drama in which he played a Greek slave named Basil. (Years later he would delight in—and wince—recalling the wooden dialogue: "Helena! Is it really you? What a joy!") In 1956 he had his first hit, playing the boxer Rocky Graziano in *Somebody Up There Likes Me,* then followed with a decade-long run that, by itself, could have been anyone else's brilliant career: *The Long, Hot Summer* (1958), *Cat on a Hot Tin Roof* (1958), *The Hustler* (1961), *Hud* (1963), *Harper* (1966) and *Cool Hand Luke* (1967). Until 1960 Warner had been paying Newman $25,000 per picture; that year he bought out his contract for $500,000; within two years he was earning $750,000 for each film. Hinting at what was to come with Newman's Own, he used some of his income to fund his No Sutch Foundation, which gave money to the NAACP and other liberal organizations. He believed passionately that everyone living in a democracy should be involved—"The people that don't vote, piss on 'em," he said bluntly—and, against the advice of some Hollywood veterans, spoke loudly for the causes he believed in. An appearance with Dr. Martin Luther King Jr. in Alabama reportedly caused his films to be pulled from local theaters.

There had been another seismic change in those early years. As Newman and actress Joanne Woodward recalled later, they first met in 1953, in an agent's office in New York City. Sparks flew, but the fire built slowly. In 1957 he and his first wife, who by then had three children, split, and he married Woodward. He didn't talk publicly about that time of his life ("It's simply nobody's business. What happened to us during that period is not gonna help anybody live a happy life"), but his and Woodward's marriage went on to become something of a national institution. The couple had three daughters, worked together often (*Rachel, Rachel,* which he directed and she starred in, was nominated for four Academy Awards) and celebrated their 50th wedding anniversary on Jan. 29, 2008.

In love with his wife he was. Publicly loquacious, about that or other personal matters? Only rarely, and when the moon was right. At the Cannes Film Festival in 1987, a journalist, trying to draw him out, asked a question that Newman had been chewing on all his life: "What does a star owe his public?" Newman, in just two words, gave an answer that spoke both of his gratitude and his lifelong battle to stay, as he called it, a free agent: "Thank you."

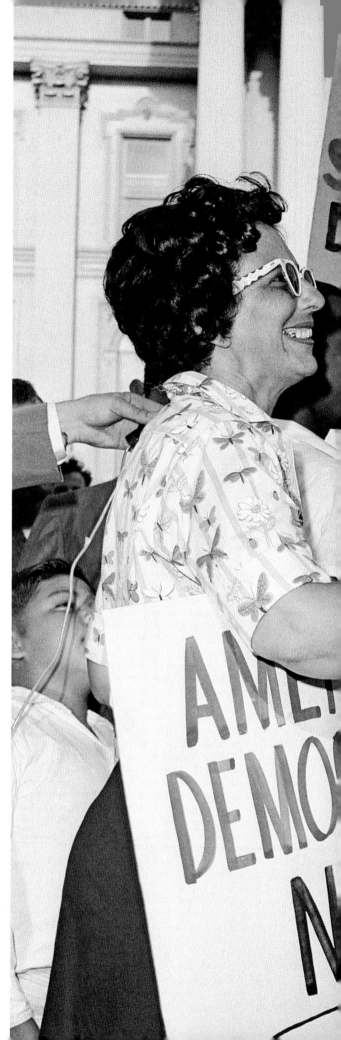

1963/A High Point
"People in Hollywood come up to me and say, 'Why take a chance? Don't make enemies,'" said Newman (with Marlon Brando at a demonstration against housing discrimination). "What they're basically asking me to do is be a person without character. . . . I prefer to make enemies." He succeeded, spectacularly: Newman was thrilled when it came to light that he had made the Top 20 on President Nixon's infamous Enemies List. "I have been fortunate in my lifetime to be tapped for a reasonable abundance of honors," he said, "but none delighted me or elevated me in the eyes of my children more than my placement as No. 19."

Joanne
& Paul

A LOVE STORY

Married for 50 years, costars in 10 movies
and best friends through thick and thin, they
were one of Hollywood's great romances

1958/Playing for Keeps

"It's certainly an exciting marriage, but I don't know that it's the Rock of Gibraltar," Newman said in 1990. "It's a very complicated thing, two people together for as long as we've been."

A

Always a little squirmy when it came to giving interviews, Paul Newman sat in the dining room of his Manhattan apartment and explained his press-shyness. "After you've answered the same questions 134 times, it's hard to come up with new answers," he said.

"And that makes me feel dull." Just then his wife—who sometimes called him Sam Superstar—swept in and sensed a cue. Said Joanne Woodward to her dazzling husband: "But you *are* dull."

She was teasing, of course, though there was some truth to what she said. For in fact Paul Newman and Joanne Woodward—who celebrated a half-century of marriage in January 2008—stripped nearly all the glamour out of their great love story, reveling instead in a simple, happy domesticity. They were at once Hollywood's most famously lasting couple—five decades in movieland, after all, is somewhere between "era" and "eon"—and, perhaps, its most private pair, shun-

ning L.A. for the woods of Connecticut, preferring throw rugs to red carpets. They seemed, in their easy and timeless rapport, to need only one thing—not roles or riches or royal treatment but, simply, each other. "He adores her," the actress Kyra Sedgwick, their costar in 1990's *Mr. & Mrs. Bridge,* said of the two. "He'll pull her down on his lap. They're openly affectionate with each other and they're both so loving and warm."

They recall first meeting in their agent's office on a scorching Manhattan day. Joanne, who would go on to win a Best Actress Oscar for *The Three Faces of Eve,* came in to cool off; Newman, in his one and only

1/At Home
"We laugh a lot,"
said Newman (with
Woodward in 1963).
2/On the Road
The couple checked
out books in '59.
3/Partners
A secret to their
marriage? "I
think we delight
in watching the
progression," said
Newman (with
Woodward in '73).
4/Just Married!
Right after their
wedding at the
Hotel El Rancho in
Las Vegas in 1958.
5/Hands On
One of the few
married couples
to be jointly
honored leave
their handprints at
Grauman's Chinese
Theater in 1963.
6/Rarely Apart
On the set of her
1968 drama *Rachel,
Rachel,* which
Newman directed.

suit, a seersucker, was introduced as a rising star. "I was wiping away the perspiration, and out steps this gorgeous Arrow Collar ad," she would recall. "I hated him." They worked together in a Broadway production of *Picnic* in 1953; six years later, after Newman's divorce from his first wife, Jackie, they wed in Las Vegas. "I had two weeks off between films," Newman explained. "We were in a hurry."

After that, they slowed things down. Together they restored an old farmhouse in Westport, Conn., and raised their three daughters there—Nell, who cofounded Newman's Own Organics; Melissa, a mother and artist; and Clea, who runs an organization that helps people with disabilities through horses and riding (he also had two daughters, Susan and Stephanie, from his first marriage). Together they weathered the 1978 death of Newman's son from his first marriage, Scott, 28, who accidentally overdosed on drugs. Newman rarely spoke about the tragedy, except to say that his son's drug problem eventually drove them apart. At the time of Scott's death, "I had lost my ability to help," Newman said. "We both backed away." The

5

6

4

1968/Home Sweet Home
Paul Newman (with Woodward and daughters Nell and Clea) tried not to sign autographs when his children were around.

pain he felt once his son was gone, he added, never went away.

There were rough spots in the marriage too—"body-bending confrontations," according to Newman. Both had to deal with his outsize fame, and Woodward—who largely backed off her career to concentrate on family—admitted to feeling "resentment." She "really gave up her career for me, to stick by me, to make the marriage work," Newman said. Sometimes their fights got so heated, he actually stormed out. "I've packed up and left a few times," he said, "and then I realized I have no place to go."

That's because they were each other's hearth and home. They worked together on 10 movies, tolerated each other's passions ("I'd trade her a couple of ballets for a couple of races," he'd say) and remained, famously, faithful. "I have steak at home. Why should I go out for hamburger?" he declared in 1968, coining the phrase—and annoying his wife, who was hardly complimented by the comparison to meat. "She's like a classy '62 Bordeaux," Newman amended in a later interview. "No, make it a '59. That's a year that ages well in the bottle. Will I get in trouble for that?"

Truth is, there wasn't much that could spoil their rare chemistry. Newman, who could be prickly, always loosened up when his wife came around, melted by her breezy, brassy charm. She, in turn, always fell for his kitchen know-how and corny jokes. "He makes me laugh and I make him laugh," Woodward said, "and that's really the best thing of all." Okay, so maybe their love affair would have made a lousy movie—all that kidding and cuddling and, yeesh, *contentment!* But as real-life romances go, theirs was, to the very end, a classic. "I don't think in my heart I ever thought we wouldn't [be together]," said Newman. "She is the last of the great broads."

1/Speed Demon
Newman and daughter Nell on the set of *Winning* in 1968.
2/New Father
To their kids, "we want to be just Mommy and Daddy," said Woodward of herself and Newman (with daughter Clea in '65).
3/Tragedy
"It never gets better," Newman said of the death of son Scott (with him in '72).
4/Kidding Around
With daughter Nell in '68.
5/Family Affair
At home in '73 with (clockwise from center left) Clea, Nell, Melissa, Stephanie and Joanne.

2002/A Marriage That Worked

"I've heard so many people say they couldn't work with their husband," Woodward once said. "I think, 'Why are you married to him then? If you can't work with him, how do you live with him?'"

> **❝** She's had many opportunities to go abroad or on location . . . and she's turned them down to stay with me **❞**

Speed Racer

Thrilled by the challenge, and the discovery he had a gift,
Newman found in racing a passion and a refuge

/Faster
"Newman has
something that
drivers can only
be born with—a soft
touch," said racing
circuit veteran
Sam Posey of the
actor (right, in
the film *Winning*).
Asked if he had a
death wish, Newman
offered a one-word
answer: "Horses---."

Why racing? "I always really wanted to be a jock," Newman explained. "I played football badly. I skied, badly. The only person I could ever dance with with any success was Joanne. I move across the dance floor like a dislocated tree trunk. And strangely, the only thing that I ever found any grace in was a car."

He fell in love with the sport while filming *Winning* in 1968. Acting was maddeningly, eternally subjective; racing, with its bright-line distinction between victory and defeat, appealed immensely to his competitive nature. "It's hard to be competitive about something as amorphous as acting," he said. "But you can be competitive in racing because the rules are very simple and the declaration of a winner is very concise." He also got a visceral charge from managing a 2,500-lb. machine with what rivals came to acknowledge was an artist's touch. "Somewhere along the line," he said, "I

like to think I went as fast as the car could go, that I went around there at the limit of my own adhesion."

Newman rose steadily in the amateur ranks and won national titles before enjoying a headline-making finish: 2nd, with his two fellow drivers, at the 24-hour Le Mans endurance race in 1979. After the race, in an indication of how much the win meant to him, Newman allowed himself an exceedingly rare public display of almost-ego: "Perhaps now people will stop taking me for a stupid actor who is simply playing at racing," he said, "and accept me as a serious racer." He didn't have to convince other drivers. Said Sam Posey: "He is now one of the top endurance racers in the world."

Newman loved the camaraderie he found at the track, and the lack of pretense. "Racing," he said, "is the best way I know to get away from all the rubbish of Hollywood."

On the car:
RACING
PAUL NEWMAN
DICK BARBOUR
ROLF STOMMELEN
70
IMSA
Toys For Big Boys

1979/
Popping the Cork
Newman with his team's Le Mans Porsche and celebrating (right) their runner-up finish. Happy at the track (left), he often arranged his acting projects around the racing season.

On the bottle: MOËT & CHANDON

The Good Guy

A Man with a Plan
"There were only two things he knew—the name of the camp and that it would be built yesterday," said Dr. Howard Pearson, Hole in the Wall's founding medical director. Newman was a regular visitor, hanging out with the kids, from day one.

It started with salad dressing—and grew into a charity empire, Newman's Own Foundation, that raised millions of dollars. But dearest to the actor's heart was his Hole in the Wall Gang camp—a wonderland for ailing children

I

It didn't seem, at first, a promising idea. "My face on a bottle of salad dressing? Not a chance in hell," said Paul Newman. The actor had long concocted homemade dressing for his family and given it, corked into old wine bottles, as gifts to friends and neighbors. In December 1980 it occurred to him that he could fill a few extra bottles, sell them and give the money to charity. But a local supermarket owner told him the only way to get anyone to *try* the product was to put the actor's mug on the merchandise—and Newman balked.

4

And then . . . he had a thought. "If we were to go the lowest of the low road and plaster my face on a bottle of oil and vinegar dressing just to line our pockets, it would stink," he told his good friend and would-be partner, writer A.E. Hotchner. "But to go the low road to get to the high road—for charity, for the common good—now *there's* an idea worth the hustle, a reciprocal trade agreement."

It worked. Newman's face went on the label, 2,000 cases went to stores, and 10,000 bottles sold in two weeks—forcing the manufacturer to put on extra shifts to keep pace. Newman and Hotchner rented a small office, installed some of Newman's patio furniture, and pinned up a sales chart. Soon the "sales" line left the chart and began climbing the

wall. Then it started moving across the ceiling. One year later sales had topped $3.2 million.

Since then, Newman's Own and its foundation have become a food and charity juggernaught, offering more than 175 products from pretzels to Fig Newmans and giving 100 percent of its profits to thousands of worthy causes. So far, Newman and his foundation have donated $250 million and counting. Newman stayed intimately involved throughout his life, from writing the quirky label copy (the lemonade promises to "restore virginity") to figuring out where to send the money. Beneficiaries have included everything from $1 million to Hurriucane Katrina survivors, to 75 refrigerated trucks for Feeding America, which services out-of-the-way communities, to a remarkable enterprise that became very close to Newman's heart: the Hole in the Wall Gang camps for kids with cancer and other life-threatening diseases. Named for the band of outlaws immortalized in his movie *Butch Cassidy and the Sundance Kid,* the camps embodied one of Newman's central philosophies. He believed "that you just have to do good," said A.E. Hotchner. "You have to be concerned about people who have less than you have." There are now 11 camps in seven countries, serving more than 11,000 kids each year.

Newman kept a cabin at the original Hole in the Wall, in northeastern Connecticut,

and would visit four or five times a summer. In the outside world, he was often exasperated by what he saw as growing greed and selfishness in American culture; one senses, in the way he talked about Hole in the Wall, that it was a place he went to find hope. "You think you've created something for kids who are not as lucky as you are," he said. "And you find out that the people who are in service to these kids are getting back more then they're giving. So those kids—the counselors, the people who work with these young children—there is where you see what the real grace of this country is, and its power, and its conscience."

I've had friends who died young. Longevity is an incredible gift and some people don't get to enjoy it "

And It All Started with Salad Dressing
Newman at Hole in the Wall Gang fundraisers with Julia Roberts (right) and George Clooney and Bruce Willis; and Paul's daughter Nell, presenting a check to a British charity.

Cool At Every

1954

1956

1957

1962

1970

1971

1972

1973

1981

1982

1983

1984

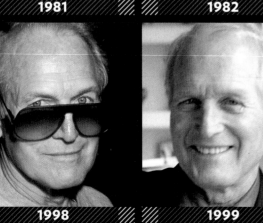
1998

1999

2000

2002

Age

Chiseled, sensual, amused, inviting, angry, beautiful, sincere—and, young or old, arresting. A memorable face, a graceful man

1963

1964

1965

1968

1975

1976

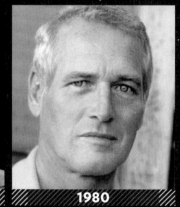
1978

1980

1987

1991

1994

1996

2003

2004

2006

2008

Career in Movies

1954/The Silver Chalice

1956/Somebody Up There Likes Me

1956/The Rack

1957/The Helen Morgan Story

1957/Until They Sail

1958/The Long, Hot Summer

1958/The Left Handed Gun

1958/Cat on a Hot Tin Roof

1958/Rally 'Round the Flag, Boys

1959/The Young Philadelphians

1960/From the Terrace

1960/Exodus

1961/The Hustler

1961/Paris Blues

1962/Sweet Bird of Youth

1962/Hemingway's Adventures of a Young Man

1963/Hud

1963/A New Kind of Love

1963/The Prize

1964/What a Way to Go

1964/The Outrage

1966/Lady L

1966/Harper

1966/Torn Curtain

1967/Hombre

1967/Cool Hand Luke

1968/The Secret War of Harry Frigg

1969/Winning

1969/Butch Cassidy and the Sundance Kid

1970/WUSA

1971/Sometimes a Great Notion

1972/Pocket Money

1972/The Life and Times of Judge Roy Bean

1973/The Mackintosh Man

1973/The Sting

1974/The Towering Inferno

1975/The Drowning Pool

1976/Buffalo Bill and the Indians

1977/Slap Shot

1979/Quintet

1980/When Time Ran Out

1981/Fort Apache, the Bronx

1981/Absence of Malice

1982/The Verdict

1984/Harry & Son

1986/The Color of Money

1989/Fat Man and Little Boy

1989/Blaze

1990/Mr. & Mrs. Bridge

1994/The Hudsucker Proxy

1994/Nobody's Fool

1998/Twilight

1999/Message in a Bottle

2000/Where the Money Is

2002/Road to Perdition

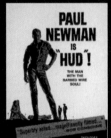

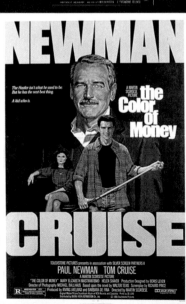

Masthead

Editor Cutler Durkee **Design Director** Sara Williams **Director of Photography** Chris Dougherty **Art Director** Cass Spencer **Photography Editor** C. Tiffany Lee-Ramos **Editorial Manager** Andrew Abrahams **Writers** Tom Gliatto, Alex Tresniowski **Reporters** Ellen Shapiro, Mary Shaughnessy, Kristen Mascia, Hugh McCarten, Lesley Messer, **Copy Editors** Ben Harte (Chief), Pearl Chen, Aura Davies, Lance Kaplan, Alan Levine, Mary Radich **Production Editors** Denise M. Doran, Ilsa Enomoto, Cynthia Miele, Daniel J. Neuburger **Scanners** Brien Foy, Stephen Pabarue **Imaging** Romeo Cifelli, Charles Guardino, Jeff Ingledue, Robert Roszkowski **Special thanks to** Robert Britton, David Barbee, Jane Bealer, Sal Covarrúbias, Margery Frohlinger, Suzy Im, Ean Sheehy, Céline Wojtala, Patrick Yang

TIME INC. HOME ENTERTAINMENT Publisher Richard Fraiman **General Manager** Steven Sandonato **Executive Director Marketing Services** Carol Pittard **Director Retail & Special Sales** Tom Mifsud **Director New Product Development** Peter Harper **Assistant Director Newsstand Marketing** Laura Adam **Assistant Director Brand Marketing** Joy Butts **Associate Counsel** Helen Wan **Book Production Manager** Suzanne Janso **Design & Prepress Manager** Anne-Michelle Gallero **Senior Brand Manager TWRS/M** Holly Oakes **SPECIAL THANKS to** Glenn Buonocore, Tymothy Byers, Susan Chodakiewicz, Margaret Hess, Brynn Joyce, Robert Marasco, Brooke Reger, Mary Sarro-Waite, Ilene Schreider, Adriana Tierno, Alex Voznesenskiy

Credits

FRONT COVER
David Sutton/MPTV

TITLE PAGE
David Sutton/MPTV

CONTENTS
MPTV

COOL
4 Bradley Smith/Corbis; **6** Neal Peters Collection; **8** Sid Avery/MPTV; **10** Neal Peters Collection; **12** Bradley Smith/Corbis; **14** Dalmas/SIPA; **16** Mark Kaufmann/Time & Life Pictures/Getty; **18** David Sutton/MPTV; **20** (from top) Everett; David Sutton/Retna; **21** Fotos International/Getty; **22** Mark Kaufmann/Time & Life Pictures/Getty

ON SCREEN
24 Bettmann/Corbis; **27** Bettmann/Corbis; **28** Photofest; **29** (clockwise from top right) Sanford Roth/AMPAS/MPTV; Everett; Photos 12/Polaris; Globe; **30** Foto Fantasies; **32** Lawrence Schiller/© Polaris Communications, Inc. (3); **33** Lawrence Schiller/© Polaris Communications, Inc.; **34** Lawrence Schiller/© Polaris Communications, Inc.; **36** Lawrence Schiller/© Polaris Communications, Inc.; **37** (clockwise from top right) Everett; John

Springer Collection/Corbis; Neal Peters Collection; Lawrence Schiller/© Polaris Communications, Inc. (2); **38** Lawrence Schiller/© Polaris Communications, Inc.; **40** Orlando/Globe; **42** Kobal; **43** (clockwise from top right) Photos 12/Polaris; SIPA; ScreenScenes; **44** (clockwise from top) Bert Stern; Everett; Globe; Everett; **45** (clockwise from top) Photos 12/Polaris; Gjon Mili/Time Life Pictures/Getty; MPTV; **46** (from top) Everett; Shooting Star; **47** Everett; **48** ScreenScenes; **49** (from top) Neal Peters Collection; ScreenScenes; **50** Globe; **52** (from top) Globe; Sid Avery/MPTV; **53** (clockwise from top) Everett; Globe; MPTV; **54** (from top) Curt Gunther/MPTV; Photofest; **55** Universal Photo/SIPA

GROWING UP
56 Everett; **57** Seth Poppel/Yearbook Library; **58** Rochelle Law/Online USA/Newscom; **59** (from top) E. Peter Schroeder/StockPhotoFinder; Eve Arnold/Magnum Photos; **60** (clockwise from top left) Everett/Everett USA; Rochelle Law/

Online USA/Newscom; Everett; Seth Poppel/Yearbook Library; **61** E. Peter Schroeder/StockPhotoFinder; **62** Time & Life Pictures/Getty; **63** Dalmas/SIPA; **64** Boccon-Gibod/SIPA; **67** AP

JOANNE AND PAUL: A LOVE STORY
68 Photo by Milton H. Greene ©2008 Joshua Greene/www.archiveimages.com; **70** Sid Avery/MPTV; **72** Sara Krulwich/The New York Times/Redux; **74** (clockwise from top) David Sutton/MPTV; Thevenin/SIPA; Gordon Parks/Time Life Pictures/Getty; **75** (clockwise from top right) Neal Peters Collection; Mark Kaufmann/Time & Life Pictures/Getty; AP; **76** Photo by Milton H. Greene ©2008 Joshua Greene/www.archiveimages.com; **78** (clockwise from top left) David Sutton/MPTV (2); Max B. Miller/Fotos International/Getty; David Sutton/MPTV; **79** Photo by Milton H. Greene ©2008 Joshua Greene/www.archiveimages.com

THE DRIVER
80 David Sutton/MPTV; **82** Ron Galella/Wireimage;

83 (clockwise from top right) Everett; Gary Lewis/Polaris; David Sutton/MPTV; Timothy White/Corbis Outline; Photo by Milton H. Greene ©2008 Joshua Greene/www.archiveimages.com; **84** (from top) Ang/Fame; Charlotte Observer/MCT/Landov; Ray Fairall/IPOL/Globe; **85** Ang/Fame; (inset) AP

THE GOOD GUY
86-87 Association of The Hole in The Wall Camps;(3); **88** (from top) Association of The Hole in The Wall Camps; Marilyn K. Yee/New York Times/Redux; Peter Booker/Rex USA; **89** CGE/Olycom/SIPA; **90** (clockwise from left) John Muggenborg; Kevin Mazur/Wireimage; Lester Cohen/Wireimage; Rex USA; **91** Granata Press/IPOL/Globe

EVERY AGE
92 1st row (from left) Everett; Lester Glassner Collection/Neal Peters; MPTV; Neal Peters Collection; 2nd row (from left) J.T./Retna; Everett; Terry O'Neill/Getty; SUS/Retna; 3rd row (from left) Gary Lewis/Polaris; Bettmann/Corbis; Ray Fairall/IPOL/Globe; Eric Heinila/Shooting

Star; 4th row(from left) Kelly Jordan/Globe; Jim Cooper/AP; Peter Booker/Rex USA; Yoram Kahana/Shooting Star; **93** 1st row (from left) Everett; AP; David Sutton/MPTV (2); 2nd row (from left) CBS/Landov; AP (2); Steve Schapiro; 3rd row (from left) Lazic/SIPA; Jerry Watson/Retna; Douglas Pizac/AP; Roussier/SIPA; 4th row (from left) Starworld Fotos; Rose M. Prouser/SIPA; INF; Paul Hurley/Polaris

CREDITS
94 Cool Hand Luke poster: Foto Fantasies; All other posters: Everett

A LAST WORD
96 Magnum Photos

BACK COVER
(clockwise from top left) Lawrence Schiller/© Polaris Communications, Inc.; Kobal; Michael O'Neill/Corbis Outline; E. Peter Schroeder/StockPhotoFinder; John Springer Collection/Corbis; Lawrence Schiller/© Polaris Communications, Inc.; Lester Glassner Collection/Neal Peters

" We are such spendthrifts with our lives. The trick of living is to slip on and off the planet with the least fuss you can muster. I'm not running for sainthood. I just happen to think that in life we need to be a little like the farmer, who puts back into the soil what he takes out "

Paul Newman
Jan. 26, 1925—Sept. 26, 2008